CALGARY

PEARL OF THE WEST

CALGARY

PEARL OF THE WEST

Text and Photographs by
GEORGE BRYBYCIN

GB PUBLISHING

Foreward

Calgary's brief, but fascinating history begins in the late 1800's when the Canadian Pacific Railway was pushing west toward the Pacific Ocean. Along the line, many small outposts were being established, opening up the Wild West for settlers.

Calgary was incorporated in 1884, around Fort Calgary, a North West Mounted Police base that was located by the confluence of the Bow and Elbow Rivers.

Before long, the area's fertile soil had attracted many settlers, and ranching became very successful in the area - making Calgary an important supply centre.

In 1914, oil was discovered in Turner Valley, to the south of Calgary. More exploration led to the major discovery of a large oilfield at Leduc, in 1947. Other such discoveries led to Calgary's becoming the oil capital of Canada, which in turn brought consistent growth and prosperity to the city.

During the 1960s and 70s, there was a boom in the oil industry and, at times, it seemed as though money grew on Calgary's trees, as the city grew into one of Canada's most important business centres. Then, as usually happens, the boom burst and, by the early 80s, stagnation and layoffs put a damper on the city's economy.

Even so, Calgary continued to grow, though more slowly, and in 1988 become the focus of the entire world as it hosted the Winter Olympic Games. The Olympics put Calgary on the world map for good, impressing everyone with its combination of down-home friendliness and world-class sophistication.

The city's annual Calgary Exhibition and Stampede had been a worldwide draw before the Olympics, but now the city itself was a draw. Based around the Stampede, and the nearby Canadian Rockies, and fueled by the positive impact of the Olympics, Calgary became an important international destination and developed a large and vibrant hospitality industry to provide world-class tourism.

Today, Calgary is a super-modern, opulent and cosmopolitan metropolis, which will soon reach a population of one million people.

* * *

As the saying goes, "a picture is worth a thousand words."

Well, yes, and no. Pictures can require brief captions to enrich their visual records. Further, to be called a book, a publication, such as this, requires text that is related to its subject.

In the past, I have gotten carried away and deviated from the subject in order to give my opinions on a wide variety of topics. The reaction? From any ten readers, I'd get ten different opinions.

Most people shy away from controversy, and do not like to talk about the more painful, negative aspects of life - in essence, sweeping things under the carpet and trying to pretend they don't exist.

How can we change things for the better if we cannot discuss them?

Well, publishing has an obligation, a duty, to inform and educate - even when it creates controversy in order to get discussion started.

Calgary is the pearl of the west; a city like no other - new, young, prosperous, and it has a great future.

There are those who say that there are two types of people: Calgarians, and those who want to be Calgarians. That may seem like arrogance, but the fact is, the city has grown to nearly 900,000 souls in barely one hundred years and continues to grow steadily. It has become home to more head offices than any other Canadian city, with the exception of Toronto.

Five years ago, I published the book "Calgary, The Stampede City and Environs." It sold 8,000 copies in hardcover. Since then, I have not done much photographic work in the city.

As I worked on this edition, I rediscovered this new, dynamic and rapidly growing city. I was impressed by the towering new skyscrapers in the downtown core, and the expansion of pathways and green areas along the Bow and Elbow Rivers, Glenmore Park and Fish Creek Park, among other areas. Redevelopment of the downtown core has upgraded some areas from "run down" to comfortable places in which to live and work.

The "Peace Grove", at the west end of the downtown area, is an absolutely lovely little park. Flanked by luxurious condos to the south, this park commemorates Calgary's 125th birthday, and the role of Canada as one of the world's peacekeepers. Next to it, believe it or not, is a sandstone Arc de Triomphe - though not as grand as the one in Paris, it is still an lovely little arch.

Although our city parks are beautiful and well maintained, it is still a city, a concrete jungle, and so we still need many more of them.

Nose Hill Park is a large, natural area that may need to be developed soon, as the growing population around it destroys the parks natural prairie vegetation by trampling it and allowing their pets to "do their business there" - and killing everything. One solution is to build pathways through the area, but the trick is to get to people to use them - and stay off the plant life. Another thing they should do is plant native trees in the lower areas of the park - a park without trees is just a big lawn.

Beaulieu Park, on 13th Avenue Southwest, is another lovely little oasis, meticulously built and landscaped with nice trees, shrubs, flowerbeds and broad sidewalks - however, many people cut across the grass and create little "sheep trails". Why can't they use the sidewalks and keep the beautiful grass beautiful? Things are constantly changing and evolving, but old habits die hard - especially harmful ones like this.

Look around, most our city's green areas have their corners trampled to death and the rest is hardly nice, or green - because we don't use the provided pathways. Grass is like the trees; it purifies the air and pleases the eye. Why don't we change our attitude and keep off the grass? Is it that much out of our way to use the sidewalks? That is what they were designed for. It's bad enough that there used to be strips of grass along the sidewalks in many areas, until they were trampled so thoroughly that the city no longer thought it cost-efficient to replant them and paved them over. Is more pavement what we really need?

Then there's the change in people's attitudes towards the senseless, and deadly, habit of smoking. In ten years, we've gone from smokers being everywhere, to smoking not being allowed in most buildings - and people have accepted it.

Is it that much harder to keep off the grass? The city spends millions of dollars of our tax money every year, to repair the damage we do to our parks. Wouldn't that money be better spent elsewhere? It could help improve our schools, hospitals, roads and policing. Wouldn't that make more sense?

There are those who are very proud that Calgary's population will soon pass the million mark, but are we all happy with that? And what are the consequences of such growth? Some are already calling Calgary a Sprawlville, a city of single-family dwellings, sprawling for miles in all directions.

In 1995, I predicted that Airdrie, Okotoks, Cochrane and Strathmore would be absorbed by Calgary, within twenty years, to form a mega-city of over 4,000 square kilometers. Well, I told you so! Calgary is expected to reach Airdrie in 2002, or 2003, and the other towns will be reached eventually.

What does this mean to Calgarians?

If one lives in north Airdrie and works in south Okotoks, that will mean a four-hour commute daily - inhaling toxic fumes the whole way. On windless days, brown clouds of pollution will linger over the city, people will die prematurely, and taxes will continue to climb in order to maintain the city's over-stretched infrastructure. The health of the city's citizens, and their standard of living, will decline substantially. Is there anything we can do to prevent this? Yes, there is.

First, Provincial Parks 10 km long and 3-4 km wide, like Fish Creek Park, but with a few lakes, could be established at the current north and south city limits.

Second, let's do as many of the world's cities have already done- let's freeze the city's boundaries at their current limits and halt any further expansion, so that small towns like Airdire and Okotoks, remain separate, small towns. About 25% of the city's properties are either empty, or ready to be redeveloped.

Imagine a city block where as few as 100 people live. Build four high-rise condo or apartment buildings, of 25-30 storeys, on each corner. As many as 4,000 people could live in comfortable, soundproof apartments with large balconies. In the center of the block, you would have enough space to build a pond and surround it with a mini-park. Not only would there be more people housed in an area with a beautiful environment, there would be no lawns to mow, no snow to shovel, heated underground parking and little chance of burglary - the maintenance costs would be far less than for houses.

What about density and noise, you may ask. You would be 40-50 meters from the next building - not 3-5 meters as in the average subdivision. If you have noisy neighbors, the building manager can have them evicted - if they ignore a fair warning, they're gone! The city could also start enforcing the noise by-laws that are already on the books. Living amid constant noise gets on one's nerves and creates stress, and, as we all know, stress kills.

Consider the alternative - subdivisions that go on forever and houses built within 3-5 meters of each other. What kind of privacy and freedom can one have in such a "dream home"? Practically none - one will be able to smell the neighbour's cooking, hear their music playing, their baby crying or their dog barking. You could also drive three hours to work, and back, every day. From your downtown condo, you could walk to work in a few minutes with no fear of traffic jams. Lengthened LRT lines, with lower, subsidized ticket prices, could futher reduce traffic jams and related stress.

Districts like Lake Bonavista, Bonaventure, McKenzie and a few others, are models of the kind of clean, healthy environments in which people can live, but only the very wealthy can afford to live on their waterfronts.

Why not do something similar for the average guy? Build a lake, say a kilometer long and 100 meters wide, and line it with twenty-five storey apartment buildings, spaced 60 meters apart. Surround them with lots of trees and other greenery and you have beautiful accommodation for up to 20,000 people - as opposed to the 400 who would live in single dwellings on the same amount of space.

Imagine the view from your 20th floor balcony: colourful canoes, ducks and geese on the lake; the reflections of beautiful buildings on the water; and best of all, the fresh air.

Is the population density too high? Not really, much of the world lives like that now, only without the lake and the greenery! All we are really talking about is stopping the urban sprawl and saving agricultural land - we have to grow our food somewhere!

Existing city lakes are round, which is a wasteful shape - we do not need oceans inside the city. The long, narrower lakes I've described would still permit all the usual watersports, including yachting, but would permit many more people to live on the waterfront, especially in well-designed high-rises.

In many places, malls are now being built in line with a new concept - to save space! They might be three storeys and have four levels of underground parking, but above them, 5 or 10, 30-storey office towers. This is a truly rational use of space.

If, along the twelve kilometers of MacLeod Trail, from Fish Creek to downtown Calgary, we were to build a series of 25-storey buildings, only two kilometers would be required to house the existing facilities. All the fast food joints could be on the ground floors, and the towers could handle parking by being built on pillars and having underground parking.

Calgary's downtown continues to grow into a more congested, traffic-unfriendly, concrete jungle. Why not build a mini-downtown in each quadrant of the city, so that people could live near their workplaces, and walk to the office.

While Calgary continues to grow rapidly, its systems of streets and thoroughfares do not. Many areas are already overly congested. 16th Avenue North experiences the worst gridlock on a regular basis. Half a solution will not be sufficient here. The only way to unplug that congestion is to widen 16th Avenue, from Barlow Trail to Sarcee Trail, to five lanes in each direction. It will be painful, and expensive, but it is the only solution - after all, this is the Trans-Canada Highway!

As I have already mentioned, in my previous "Calgary" book, I commented on a wide range of subjects, in a very blunt manner. After she had read it, one young lady told me, "You must really hate this city!" I was puzzled and devastated. If I hated the city, I would not have lived here for so long. So, young lady, I do love Calgary. It is my home. Only people who are complacent and unseeing do not criticize.

Calgary is a great place to live, but as the world changes, so does Calgary. Thirty years ago, we didn't have to lock our doors at night, or when going to work. Recently, my place, with two locks on the door, was broken into - as was my van. We have all heard of people whose homes were broken into twice a year, or more.

Obviously, not everything is well in paradise. Shouldn't we talk about it, or even better, do something about it? The police and the courts do very little to discourage such behaviour. In such cases, the culprit is seldom caught. When he is, we're told "he's the child of a single mother - so what can we do about it?"

Do children have the right to burglarize, or vandalize, without fear of punishment? Isn't it time we scrapped, or revised the ridiculous Young Offenders' Act that is responsible for creating and protecting young criminals, and put those criminals where they belong - correctional facilities, boot camps, or jail?

Shouldn't we recognize that young children are not born with the capacity to tell right from wrong? Shouldn't we be teaching them these things, and making sure that they understand?

Criminals are not born. They grow as a result of small rebellions that go unpunished, and progress quickly from that point on: rowdy behaviour, stealing popcorn or candy, taking money from a parent's purse/wallet, breaking and entering, stealing cars, assault, muggings, murder... When you punish children, properly, for minor offences, like stealing candy, or any other childhood rebellion, they will usually get the message and straighten out. Failing to intervene this early, makes a rapid progression to worse behaviour inevitable, and most likely, irreversible. Adult criminals are not usually rehabilitated, and an immense amount of money is spent making the effort.

One wonders why our lawmakers cannot grasp this simple principle and send parents who do discipline their children, to jail?

One last item that is worth mentioning, is the attitude of some towards needless consumerism. People are told daily, by commercials, that they need to buy more, buy everything - that is the only way to go. Production of *anything* requires raw materials and energy. Many products that cost too little, are also made too poorly and need replacing far too soon - while the now useless original item winds up in the garbage. Such excessive and careless consumerism causes mountains of garbage and pollution.

It would be educational if everyone, especially children, were to take a field trip to the municipal landfill/garbage dump. Just as smokers, who visit a terminal cancer ward, learn about the real world, and the way things really work, a visit to the dump would show you that the garbage doesn't just vanish after the garbage truck takes it away. Instead, it stays here, within a few miles of us, polluting our air, soil and water, as well ourselves. The more we consume, the more damage we are doing to ourselves - and our environment. This should be incentive enough for us to not buy like a drunken sailor, just because a TV commercial said we should. It should also be incentive for us to recycle everything that we can recycle.

Well, then, it's a fine sunny day here in Calgary - time to go for a healthy, invigorating 5-kilometer walk along the Bow River - to stay fit and happy...

Above: *T*he all-new complex of super-condominiums at the west end of Downtown, by the Bow River, The new architectural design, vivid colour and the best material combine to make for a comfortable living.

Left: *T*he tallest structure in town, at 52 storeys, the Petro-Canada Office Tower is one of Calgary's most prestigious business addresses.

Page 7: *T*his interesting new addition to Downtown is located at 5th Ave. and 1st St. S.W. The green glass facade corresponds nicely with the little green park in front of the building.

Pages 8 & 9: *T*he Central part of Downtown, Prince's Island Park and the Bow River as seen from the north hill above Sunnyside.

Above: A *"warm" winter image of the Bow River and the Louise Bridge, which links Downtown with the Hillhurst District. At -25° C, a crisp February sunset.*

Left: T*he lofty and imposing Canterra Tower, next to Prince's Island Park and its facilities, dominates the north end of Downtown.*

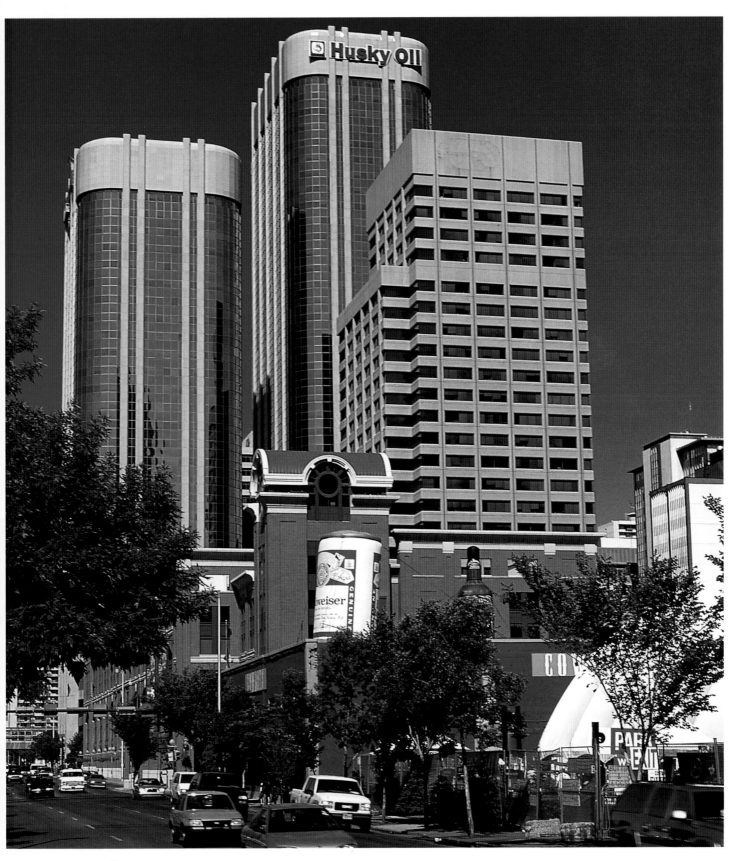

Above: *I*mposing office towers along 9 Ave. S.W. This is the oil capital of Canada, with all its wealth and power.

Left Upper: *T*his has got to be the loveliest little park in the whole world. Prince's Island has got it all: strolling, jogging, cycling, and tanning - even the geese feel at home here.

Left Lower: *E*au Claire, adjacent to the solid wall of downtown, is the hub for all sorts of activities: shopping, dining, movies - and there's even a wading pool for the kids.

Above: *A* *beautiful, green oasis next to the bustling Downtown - the Prince's Island Lagoon - at its best.*

Left: *T*he *Government of Alberta Southern Offices are surrounded by a cozy, but elegant park. Across 5th Ave. S.W., stands a tall, modern office tower.*

*T*he sandstone Government of Alberta Southern Offices, in the heart of downtown, were once McDougall School. It is a serene place to spend one's lunch hour.

19

This footbridge over the Bow River links Downtown with the Sunnyside Community. Downtown buildings rise over golden October poplars on a pleasant autumn day.

Above: ***B***uilt for the 1988 Winter Olympics, the Calgary Saddledome is a technological and architectural marvel. It is home to The Calgary Flames Hockey Club, as well as a host of sporting and entertainment events.

Left: ***M***eticulously constructed by the best Chinese artisans, The Chinese Cultural Center graces the heart of Chinatown, in the shadow of the opulent Calgary business district.

*R*egardless of global warming, Calgary still gets its share of winter hardships. Above is the Center Street Bridge, spanning the Bow River and the icy cold Memorial Drive.

*O*n the left, is a gloomy and scary looking Downtown, as viewed from Scotchman's Hill, on a December morning when daylight lasts for only 8 hours, and temperatures plummet to -30°C.

Above: A *little smaller than the Arc de Triomphe in Paris, this sandstone arch is located in the lovely park along the Bow River, just west of Downtown, where all those fancy, comfortable condos were built, recently.*

Left: K*ensington Gate, a fancy building on Westmount Boulevard, by the Louise Bridge. These colourful flowerbeds are part of the Bow River Parks and Pathways system.*

Pages 24-25: A *stunning view of Downtown as photographed from Petro-Canada Tower. The view encompasses the entire western part of the city, the Bow River and the gorgeous Rocky Mountain chain.*

Above: The beautiful and elegant Prince's Island Park is a green oasis situated next to the bustling Downtown and Eau Claire.

Left: Calgary is the energy capital of Canada, and a major business Centre. This is where most oil companies have their head offices. Because of the prohibitive cost of land, only tall towers are feasible to build.

*C*algary's winters can be long and harsh, but the area is blessed with Chinooks - warm west winds that come over the Rockies, from the Pacific Ocean, causing milder temperatures for days on end. This is such a morning in Mount Royal.

*O*lympic Plaza, which was built for the 1988 Olympics, has become a people place - where people meet, play or relax. In the winter, the Plaza becomes a skating rink.

Above: **C**algary's frequently changing weather causes dramatic skies, with unique cloud formations and fantastic displays of lightning and rainbows.

Left: **C**algary is a city of festivals and joyous fun. The Calgary Stampede is billed as "The Greatest Outdoor Show On Earth". Impressive fireworks end each day of the Stampede.

*O*n the corner of 8th Avenue & 8th Street S.W., nestles a little green area called Century Gardens. With its many trees and sculptures, and a pond with a waterfall, it has a cozy, homey ambience. It is a lovely place to spend one's lunch hour, or just some time relaxing in the shade of a gorgeous tree.

*R*ight in the heart of Downtown, this little park was created on a vacant piece of land. With the addition of just a few trees, flowerbeds and some benches to sit on, the harshness of the concrete jungle is softened. Trees mean life, health and well-being.

Above: *F*rom the other side, this impressive glass and aluminum structure looks like an ocean-going ship. In front of the building, located at 8th St. and 8th Ave. S.W., is a cozy park, Century Gardens with a pond and fancy greenery. It is a popular place with the lunch crowd.

Left Upper: *T*his new subdivision of McKenzie is 18 kilometers from Downtown. With its large lake, and broad, treed streets it makes for a nice suburban living. Driving Downtown, to work, is another story.

Left Lower: *G*lenmore Reservoir needs no introduction. Calgary's source of drinking water, this 5-km lake was created by damming the Elbow River. All sorts of watersports are allowed on the lake - the presence of people and pets causes the city to use more and more chlorine to keep the water "drinkable and healthy". (Many cities keep their sources of drinking water fenced off from human access.) Heritage Park on the right.

Calgary's skyline gets more impressive by the minute. Boom or bust, the city just continues to grow. Many of the newest buildings showcase the most up-to-date architectural design and materials. In particular, using coloured glass and facades creates a pleasant, livable impression. Incorporating a lot of green spaces into the city organism, makes it a concrete jungle with heart.

*N*ot that long ago, Chestermere Lake was a picturesque place, located 20 km east of downtown Calgary. There were a few dozen small summer cottages, clean water and a peaceful ambience. Today, nearly the entire shore is lined with large houses. On the west side this is... a city, with large houses, streets a golf course, stores and, you name it... The Lake itself, is as busy as Hong Kong's harbour. All sorts of watercraft can be seen and heard here. Rules? It seems to be 'do as you please!' Young people drive speedboats and water skidoos at high speeds, causing accidents. Other than that, the lake is a great recreational area.

*T*he lovely Lake Sikome is located at the east end of Fish Creek Provincial Park, next to the Bow River. Not long ago, the park was south of Calgary. Today the city (Sprawlville) has already crossed Highway 22X on its quick march towards Okotoks. This picturesque, artificial lake is a swimming mecca designed for families, and is open to everyone. The water is not too deep; there are plenty of sandy beaches, and lifeguards are on duty - making this a very popular recreational area. The lake's basic facilities include: a snack bar, drinks, ice cream and rest rooms. Take MacLeod Trail South and, at Sunvalley Boulevard, go about 4 km east, and there you are...

*T*he West End of Downtown, an apartment and condo district, reflects its sunny faces in the Bow River. The one on the right resembles a modern Chateau on the French Riviera - beautiful.

*T*he newly renovated Center Street Bridge glitters, richly illuminated by decorative lighting. The bridge links Downtown with the northern part of the city. Reversible lanes make rush hour traffic less congested.

*C*algary, with its world-class facilities, is a major sports center. *T*he city hosts professional hockey, football and baseball clubs - as well as many other sports, on various levels. *A* football game in progress at McMahon Stadium.

*S*ome major ski competitions were staged at the former Paskapoo, during the 1988 Winter Olympics. Now, Canada Olympic Park, at the West End of the city, by the Trans-Canada Highway, is a major winter sports complex.

A frigid and frosty February night falls over Calgary's Downtown - as photographed from Knob Hill, just west of city centre.

A splendid midsummer's image of the impressive east end of Downtown - with the city's premier landmark, the Calgary Tower, as viewed from Scotchman's Hill.

*Y*ee-Hah! It is Stampede time in Calgary - when many Calgarians exchange their three-piece suits for blue jeans and cowboy hats. The Calgary Stampede begins on the first Friday of July and runs for ten days - over one million people attend, annually. It is "the greatest outdoor show on earth," and good, clean fun for all.

*Left: B*y nature, cowboys love to ride horses. If a horse is not at hand, they will ride almost anything - even a locomotive. The gold and silver Bankers Hall Towers provide an impressive backdrop.

Above: *T*he Calgary Stampede is mostly run by hundreds of devoted volunteers, who perform all sorts of duties with pride and a friendly smile.

Left: *A* new addition to downtown Calgary - a 4.5-star hotel with pretty blue windows and elegant modern architecture.

Upper: *An old tradition - breakfast is served throughout the city during the ten days of Stampede. The breakfasts are sponsored by various companies and organizations and may include: pancakes, bacon, sausage and coffee. Some fancier ones include grapes and strawberries.*

Lower: *To keep its Olympic spirit alive, Calgary stages a Winter Festival to celebrate winter sports and fun.*

Left: *The Stampede is so many things. Over 100,000 people visit the grounds most days - watching the rodeo and chuckwagon races; stage shows and concerts; the Indian Village, or enjoying various rides on the midway, along with exotic foods and drinks.*

Above: A*t the Stampede, anything is possible - one can even "Rise and shine with Ralph". The popular Premier of Alberta attends a Stampede breakfast, serves a few pancakes, shakes a few hands, makes a brief speech and poses for a few pictures, with the Stampede Queen and Princesses - much to everyone's delight.*

Left: T*he vibrant, lively Stephen Avenue is a real people place. It is the only stretch of Downtown where historic buildings are meticulously maintained amidst the expanse of modern towers.*

Above: **O**ne of the most breathtaking, dangerous Stampede events - the Chuckwagon Races.

Left: **O**ne of the Stampede's biggest attractions, especially with foreign visitors, is The Indian Village. Native Canadians live in tepees on the grounds, and allow visitors to enter. They also re-enact many traditional rites and dances - to the delight of all.

Above: *C*harming young cowgirls pose, with their great Tennessee walking horse, on the Stephen Avenue Mall.

Left: *T*he Stampede's Midway is a big barrel of fun for everyone. The high, fast rides are especially enjoyed by the young.

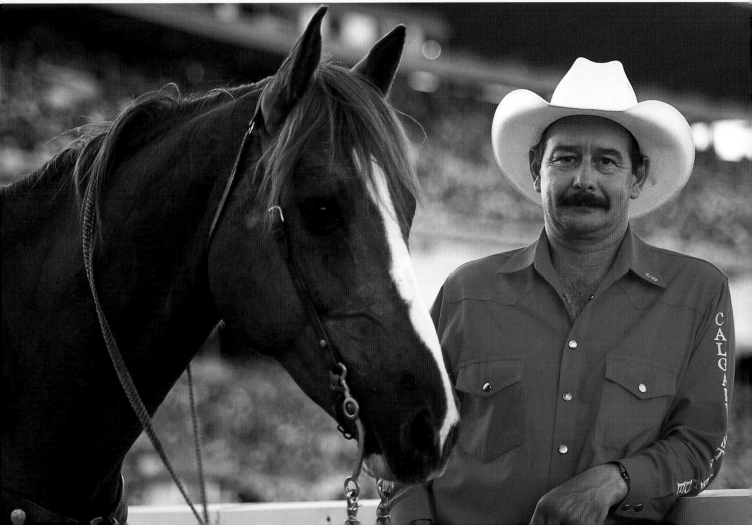

Above: A *place for bestowing fame and glory: The Olympic Plaza is where the medals were awarded during the 1988 Winter Olympics. Today it is a place for many activities, and a park where one can sit under a tree and relax. Notice the beauty of these tall blue spruce and elm trees.*

Page 60: S*tampede horsemen, officials and organizers - a happy crew, having fun.*

Page 61: Upper: A *Canadian country music legend - Ian Tyson, at his Alberta ranch.*

Lower: A *chuckwagon outrider and his "thinking horse", a really intelligent beast.*

The Stampede Queen and Princesses are not hereditary royalty. They are chosen, each year, from dozens of young ladies who aspire to the title. They are not judged purely for their beauty, but also for their knowledge of the Stampede, their riding skills and their ability to speak in public. These lovely ladies are the Royalty of the 2001 Stampede.

A stampede is the sudden rush of a panic-stricken herd. One of the most exciting Stampede competitions is Bareback Bronc Riding. Not many cowboys survive the wild horse ride with their hats on. Many eat dust, or are kicked by their enraged, bucking horse.

Upper: *O*ops! *This one just got away. Calf-roping requires skill and speed.*

Lower: *S*teer *wrestling requires real skill and agility from a cowboy.*

*T*he first half of July is the time to see yellow fields of Canola throughout the southern Prairies. Canola seeds provide a valuable oil that is good for cooking and a source of "good" fats. Here we see a sprawling Canola field just south of Calgary with the majestic Rocky Mountains on the western horizon.

Long ago, the city of Calgary decided that Nose Hills, just north of the city, should be saved from development, to preserve the original Prairie vegetation and wildlife. Today, the ever-shrinking hills are entirely surrounded by the city. Thousands of people visit the 10 square-kilometer park, and since there are no official walking trails, they make their own - all over the park. Today, little flora remains undisturbed and one hardly sees any fauna at all. Free-running dogs have killed most of the birds and rodents, and bicyclists tear the fragile vegetation to bits. Both should be banned from the park. It would be wise for the city to quickly find financing to pave walking trails and convince, or force, people to use them; and reclaim the areas devastated by human activity. On lower elevations, native trees could be planted. If people would get out of the bad habit of walking on the grass, perhaps nature would then find a way to recover and prosper.

*O*il is as synonymous with Alberta as shamrocks are with Ireland. The prosperity of the Province greatly depends on its large oil and gas deposits. The energy sector employs thousands of well-paid workers, which also keeps the Province prosperous. This typical oil pump is on the Longview oil field along the foothills, in the heart of Alberta's ranching country.

69

*T*his gently rolling landscape, northeast of Calgary, is typical of this part
of the Province - the north and east are flat. The Prairies are renowned
for their spectacular sunsets - this harvest moon corresponds well with the
wheat harvest, another source of Alberta's wealth.

Above: T*his vintage photo is over 30 years old and illustrates the sun doing as it always does, rises and sets - though not always in such a glorious fashion. This photo presents the Trans-Canada Highway west of Calgary, with the jagged Rocky Mountains on the horizon.*

Left Upper: A*s the city's skyscrapers grow more plentiful, and ever higher, the Grain Elevator is simply vanishing from the scene. New and different ways of storing and marketing grain, have rendered grain elevators uneconomical and obsolete.*

Left lower: C*anadian farms are prosperous thanks to their large size and efficient, modern farming methods. The Canadian farmer frequently holds a degree in a related field, works from a computerized office and keeps up with the newest trends in agriculture. These massive feed silos are located near Stavely, south of Calgary.*

*C*algarians are blessed with great outdoor areas all around the city. There are great rivers and lakes for swimming, canoeing, yachting or fishing. A one-hour drive brings one to mighty mountains, with unlimited recreational possibilities year-round: hiking, climbing, and skiing, to name a few. Above is the one and only Lake Louise - a world-class resort west of Banff. On the left is an image of a majestic golden autumn near Banff, with Mount Rundle (2998m) dominating the scene.

*E*xcept for the month of January, winter in the Rockies is not as cold as it once was (global warming).
-40° C is now a rarity and the milder -20° C prevails. Come February and March, the mercury rises a few
more degrees, so skiing is very pleasant. Above is Second Vermilion Lake, near Banff. On the left is the
emerald-blue Lake Louise and Fairview Mountain, photographed from Little Beehive.

Above: Many label *The Valley of the Ten Peaks and Moraine Lake the pearl of The Rockies, which seems to be a correct assumption. Mt. Babel (3101m) dominates the photo, and bright fireweed adds extra spice to this magnificent scenery.*

On the left is another emerald jewel – Lower Waterfowl Lake, and further, Chephren Lake, at the foot of Howse Peak (3290m). Banff National Park.

Calgary - Heart of the New West
FACTS

Calgary was incorporated in 1884 and is now the fifth-largest city in Canada with an area of 721 square km and a population of about 883,000, as of January 2002.

Location: South-Central Alberta east of the Rockies, at the junction of the Bow and Elbow Rivers ∗ Elevation: 1,139 meters above sea level ∗ Dollar value of building permits: $2 billion Canadian, in 2000 ∗ Major parks: 29 ∗ Total area of parks in 2000: 7,822 hectares ∗ Schools (kindergarten to high school): 408 ∗ Libraries: 16 ∗ Major Daily Newspapers: 4 ∗ Radio Stations: 14 ∗ Television Stations: 7 ∗ Hospitals: 4 ∗ Museums: 16 ∗ Theatres: 30 ∗ Bookstores: 62 ∗ Theme song: Neighbours of the World (B. Bowman, T. Loney) ∗ Flower: Red Pasque Flower

Weather:Daily mean temperature, in Degrees Celsius: January -9.6, February -6.3, March -2.5, April 4.1, May 9.7, June 14.0, July 16.4, August 15.7, September 10.6, October 5.7, November -3.0, December -8.3, Year 3.9

Rainfall (in millimeters): January 0.2, February 0.2, March 1.5, April 9.2, May 43.9, June 76.7, July 69.9, August 48.7, September 42.7, October 6.4, November 0.6, December 0.1 Year 300.3

Snowfall (in millimeters): January 18.0, February 14.9, March 18.7, April 20.4, May 10.2, June 0.3, July 0.0, August 0.0, September 6.4, October 11.5, November 16.0, December 19.0, Year 135.4

Sunshine (hours per month): January 113.8, February 136.8, March 174.0, April 214.8, May 256.0, June 285.5, July 320.1, August 284.8, September 201.8, October 179.0, November 125.4, December 102.5, Year 2394.6

Average Windspeed (Kilometers per hour): Year 16 (May being the windiest month, at 18).

Maximum Temperatures: July 25, 1933 36.1° C   Minimum Temperatures: February 4, 1893 -45.0° C

Greatest 24-hour rainfall : 95.3mm   Greatest 24-hour snowfall: 48.4mm

Calgary is policed by 1,345 officers and averages 17 homicides annually.

Left: *This interesting new sculpture on the Stephen Avenue Mall, is called "The Trees". 'Planted' where once were real, shade-giving trees, these steel, man- made versions provide what, exactly? Apparently it cost several million dollars to build – money which could have paid for the planting of up to 200,000 real trees – trees that the city really needs.*

The Author

George Brybycin is a Calgary photographer who has photographed this splendid city for over 30 years, with love, passion and professionalism. This edition is his sixth volume on Calgary. He is also a renowned mountaineer, and his exploration of the Rockies has produced twenty five publications on these gorgeous mountains.

George is a perfectionist and a man of principles, who stands for many things and, as a result, often feels like he was relocated here from another, remote planet. The principles and values with which he was raised, do not exist anymore. Today everything is about money, and lots more of it.

George moves in exactly the opposite direction - the more others want, the less he wants. He genuinely believes that a person's values and morals are what count - not a person's possessions.

Some say that his values and behaviour are weird - but one is raised to be gentle, sensitive and respectful - or rough and selfish. It may seem like fiction to some of you, but in his twenties, when George was dating ladies, he sometimes stayed late - after midnight. In order not to disturb, or wake the neighbours, he would park his car at the top of a parking lot, so he could quietly roll his car into the street, in neutral, before starting the engine.

Well, there aren't people like that today. It seems that most young people today, are as inconsiderate and noisy as possible, and have no concept of discipline, or law. That might be one reason why George climbs remote mountains, far from "civilization" - to be surrounded by nature's gentle beauty, and get some peace and quiet!

George does not smoke, drink, or drug himself silly - he prefers the simple, older ways. He is a bit of a masochist - bivouacking on mountaintops can be quite dangerous, and painful. He believes in living on the edge - literally!

He also hesitates to help lazy panhandlers, who refuse to work - but when he has a few extra dollars, he donates them to Calgary's tree-planting program every year. To date, thanks to George's wisdom, the city is greener by 2500 trees.

And now, guess what? George is not getting any younger - nonetheless, it does not slow him down much. As always, he photographs Calgary, and his beloved Rockies, with passion and energy. We may expect more of his work in the form of new books.

George also writes on many, often unpopular subjects and issues. Why? To bring them into the open so that they may be discussed and improvements made. Sweeping problems under the carpet will not help anyone.

If you love humanity, and this planet, get involved - care for, and be friendly to your environment.

This book was created in Alberta by Albertans
Printed in Hong Kong, China
Text Editor: Sheldon Wiebe
Design: George Brybycin
Typesetting: K & H United Co.
First Edition: 2002 Hard Cover
Copyright © 2002 by GB Publishing
All rights reserved

No parts of this book may be reproduced in any form without written permission from the publisher, except for brief passages quoted by a reviewer.

ISBN 0-919029-32-9

This is George Brybycin's 31st book.

For current list, please write to:

GB PUBLISHING, Box 6292, Station D,
Calgary, Alberta Canada T2P 2C9

George Brybycin's collection of 20,000 35mm colour slides is FOR SALE.
Subjects include: The Rockies, Western and Northern Canada, Calgary, The 1988 Olympics, Alaska, The Western U.S. and the World (Paris, London). Also available is the collection of all 31 George's books. Offers may be tendered to GB Publishing at the address above.

Supercharging The Life of Owen

There are strange things done in the Prairie sun
By the men who surf the web;
And cyberspace is full of secret places
That would stand your hair on end;
The moonlit nights have seen queer sights,
But the queerest they've ever known;
Was the night his computer, turned electrocuter,
And supercharged life for Owen

Now Owen grew up at Shawnee Slopes
    Where the golf ball zings and rolls;
Why he gave up the good life to take him a wife...
    - God only knows;
For he was grown, and he'd left home
    Got his computer degree;
Moved in with two friends, had money to spend
    His Life was fun and carefree.

They could party all night and live the high life
    With not a care in the world;
Cook their own dinner, order it in, or
    Go out for something at Earl's; [1]
No one to say "do it this way"!
    Or "you need to clean up your room";
No broom, no shovel, and you don't get in trouble
    If you sleep till half past noon.

And girls would come and there were some
     Owen thought he would like to know;
But they were shallow, and he, a serious fellow,
     Thought them a bunch of bimbo's;
"Besides who needs a wife, I don't need the strife.
     And what could she do for me?
I can clean the nook and I'm a fine cook,
     I started before I was three!"

Owen focused on work, he's no office clerk,
     But a programmer extraordinaire;
His computer and he were quite a team
     When they were brought to bear;
When there was a problem, the boss'd take it to Owen,
     Saying "He can solve it I bet;
It may not work now, but he'll fix it somehow;
     He's the best that I've seen yet."

Sometimes at a glance he seemed in a trance
     As he concentrated so;
Eyes on the screen, mind quick and keen,
     The ideas just seemed to flow;
It seemed like a trick, he was so quick;
     He was surely one of a kind;
And there was a bet, though it wasn't proved yet,
     The computer could read his mind.

So up the ladder he rose and was happy he supposed
     Though with one thing he did wrestle;
He thought once or twice, "wouldn't it be nice
     To share life with someone special";
"But I'm not going to bond with some run of the mill blond –.
     All you get is what you see;
She's got to be smart, not some jam tart.
     Someone... kind of like me."

As time went on, no one right came along
        But he kept his standards high;
"If I get it wrong, my life is gone,
        And I'd almost rather die"

Then one night in the dark he awoke with a start:
        On the far side of the room;
His computer lay bathed in the pale rays
        of a yellow harvest moon.
He rubbed his eyes, for to his surprise,
        The thing was already on;
And a web page flashed, with a promise that,
        Caught his i-ma-gi-na-tion.

It could find you a date or a lifemate,
        And it came with a guarantee.
If you ran your request without success
        You could do your search for free.
He looked at it, and he thought a bit,
        And his thoughts turned t'ward his mother;
"If it could find that special kind,
        This might be worth the bother"

Then on impulse, Owen laughed to himself
        "I'll fool this thing – put it to shame;
There's really no risk; they just don't exist
        – I'll ask for a blond with brains"!
His request entered in, he hit send;
        Then the room seemed to darker grow;
The full moon was instead, turned dark blood red,
        Full cloaked in the earth's shadow. (2)

This startled Owen; was it a bad omen?
      Something just didn't seem right;
He reached for the mouse - he'd best get out
      Of this strange and fearsome site;
There's something wrong when things turn on
      By themselves in the dark of the night.

He clicked on close and no one knows
      Why the computer wouldn't respond;
The escape key ... control-alt-delete...
      Nothing would make it shut down;
So he shut off the power but it whirred even louder;
      Then he got a powerful jolt,
When he reached for the plug, to give it a tug,
      Of seventy million volts!

He crashed to the floor with such a roar
      That his roommates leapt from their beds;
There he lay in his room in the smoke and gloom,
      And they wondered if he were dead.
Sparks flew everywhere, and cracked in the air,
      And his whole body seemed to glow;
He was black as soot and he twitched and shook...
      What to do? They didn't know.

Then slowly he stood, like a drunkard would,
      With a bit of a tilt and sway;
His eyes were wide and the dark could not hide,
      That his mind was far, far away;
They fell back in awe, and then they saw
      The source of all this din;
Of his own accord, he clutched the cord
      That plugged the computer in.

They lunged toward that hateful cord
      To safety they gave no heed;
They had to pull that plug from the wall
      And do it with utmost speed;
In a voice quite his own, that deep baritone,
      Owen bade them relax;
"She's right here, can't you see 'er"
      And it stopped them in their tracks.

They looked around, not a soul to be found.
      It was becoming clear to them;
He'd left his brain in some cyberplane,
      When he began to speak again:
"She's really cool, she's going to school
      Taking Speech Pathology;
And that's not all cause on her wall
      Is an honours Physics degree.

Above all I find she's caring and kind;
      It's the kids she wants to teach;
Some to play the piano the way
      She'll help others with their speech.
And I can see she's made for me;
      I'm going to win her affection;
It feels so real, so here's the deal;
      Don't you break that connection.

Mom always said, blond, brunette or red,
      When true love came a knocking;
That there would be 'e-lec-tri-ci-ty'.
      And this... girl... is shocking"!

There are strange things done in the Prairie sun,
*   By the men who surf the web;*
And cyberapace is full of secret places
*   That would stand your hair on end.*
The moonlit nights have seen queer sights,
*   But the queerest they've ever known,*
Was the night his computer, turned electrocuter,
*   And Supercharged life for Owen.*

Ken Fast, Dec. 2006

(1)   Owen worked as a cook at Earls Restaurant

(2)   During a total lunar eclipse the moon takes on a dull 'blood' red colour.

After *The Cremation of Sam McGee*, by Robert Service.